THE RITUALS

Simple
Practices
to Cultivate
Well-Being,
Deepen
Relationships,
and Discover
Your True
Purpose

NATALIE MACNEIL

ILLUSTRATIONS BY LINDSAY HINE

CHRONICLE BOOKS
SAN FRANCISCO

Library of Congress Cataloging-in-Publication Data available.

ISBN 978-1-4521-8067-0

Manufactured in China.

Design by Vanessa Dina.
Illustrations by Lindsay Hine.
Typesetting by Frank Brayton.

10 9 8 7 6 5 4 3 2

Chronicle Books LLC
680 Second Street
San Francisco, CA 94107
www.chroniclebooks.com

You're invited
to an enchanted world
a space between spaces
past and future unfurl
to be reborn from cosmic dust
baptized in the River Yin
to let your wild soul dance
like raindrops in the wind
to tune in to the faded station
our ancestors still play
to make splendid sandcastles
from the grains of your days
to explore your every dimension
feel what is rapturously true

You're invited, dear one,
to the ritual that is You

INTRODUCTION

A RETURN TO RITUALS

I danced along the edge of the lush green rice fields as a choir of roosters, cicadas, and cows welcomed the sunrise over Bali. The sweet scents of frangipani and incense floated across the expansive property as a Balinese woman placed tiny, beautiful arrangements on the ground as the daily *canang sari* offering, a sacred Hindu ritual.

I paused for a moment to take it all in. I felt so peaceful, so grateful, so awestruck, as I inhaled and exhaled with all of life. I hadn't felt that way in a long time.

I had returned to the island of Bali to rest my bones and nourish my soul. I was exhausted and burnt out following a busy year that included two book launches, extraordinary personal and business growth, and a big move to a new country. Throughout that time, my main focus had been on productivity and structure so that I could stay on top of my never-ending to-do list. I had adopted the habits that I believed would make me a more "effective person."

I followed the morning routines and practices of the most successful CEOs and leaders. I read books about nutrition, habits, and exercises for high performance. If it could help me get more done, I was in.

I was hyper-productive. But the more I focused on achieving and doing, the more I felt like I'd been set adrift.

I was methodically going through my routines, checking things off my to-do lists, and accomplishing so much, but along the way I felt my joy dissipating. It felt robotic to move through each of my routines without having to think about them anymore, which had been the whole point. The nature of a habit is unconscious—we form habits by consciously repeating something until it becomes second nature, which of course has many benefits when those actions and behaviors are positive ones. But one of the drawbacks is the sort of mindless, going-through-the-motions feeling I was experiencing.

Feeling so disconnected got me thinking about the moments in my life when I feel the happiest, most energized, and in a state of flow—the feeling of total alignment and ease with every-thing I am doing and creating. Those flow states are further amplified when I'm traveling and out of my day-to-day routines, experiencing a way of being that is contrary to the stress-filled, fast-paced lifestyle so many of us are trapped in.

Chanting at the top of my lungs as sweat and tears poured down me in a new moon temazcal ritual with a Mayan shaman in Mexico.

Dancing in a ceremony in Tanzania, feeling like liquid light was coursing through my body.

Hiking among the redwoods and sequoias, communing with nature in the beautiful state of California.

Drumming and letting every beat move through me at the Venice Beach Drum Circle.

Surrendering as a local medicine woman set herbs on fire around my body as I lay on a stone in a Peruvian jungle.

Awakening during a resonant bell ritual with monks at a monastery in China.

Embodying the highest sense of aliveness I'd ever experienced while watching a body burn on a pyre at a Balinese cremation ceremony.

Fully embracing every aspect of this human experience at Burning Man in the Black Rock Desert.

I realized that every tingling-from-head-to-toe moment I could remember in my life had the same thing in common: ritual.

Rituals connect us to our needs and desires, to each other, to the earth, to other cultures, to our collective past and future, and to our curiosity around who we are and what we're doing here. Rituals are a concept as old as humanity, with the earliest known ritual dating back some seventy thousand years.

Getting lost in rich cultural traditions and powerful rituals has helped me find myself. We are missing so much when we don't open ourselves to new, enriching opportunities. How I experience the world is how I experience myself. Every new place I've been, every new stranger I've met, every new ritual I've tried, has taken me to new places within me.

The intention of this book is to guide you to new places within yourself.

I've been privileged to travel the world and have the opportunity to immerse myself in beautiful cultures and rich experiences. And this book is infused with the energy of the places

I wrote it in: Bali, Brazil, Ecuador, Chile, Los Angeles, New York, England, Canada, Mexico, Japan, Zimbabwe, Namibia, and South Africa.

But you don't need to travel far to discover a world of magic—the rituals in this book are designed to be accessible to anyone, anywhere.

In today's world, much of the sacred wisdom of rituals has been lost. Many of us are completely disconnected from the rituals that our ancestors practiced for centuries. Ideological shifts and dominant cultures have tried to erase ancient and native practices that have so much to teach us. I have deep reverence for the rituals that I have been invited to participate in by people in countries I have traveled to, and while some will be referenced in this book, I will not be sharing the practices of groups that have been oppressed and persecuted within the countries they live. That is not my place.

I am not an expert on rituals, but rather a humble and curious student committed to learning and exploring as much as I can in my lifetime. I invite you to research and further discover practices I reference, and I encourage you to explore the rituals of your own lineage. With the rise of accessible genetic testing, there's never been a better time to uncover, reconnect to, and celebrate your roots.

To practice your own rituals, and those of your ancestors, is not only an act of self-love—it can also be an act of connection, expression, divinity, and reverence. Rituals are small acts of rebellion against the systems we live in that want us to conform, to always be chasing the "bigger and better" thing, and to be the most productive cogs we can be.

Life is not about checking off a to-do list and going through the motions. Life is about living, expressing ourselves unapologetically, and spending time reveling in the people and experiences we consider most precious, the ones that give us access to our fullest potential. Those are the very things rituals celebrate.

And this is exactly why I wrote this book.

Inside these pages, I've included a rainbow of rituals for you to sample, from the ancient to the new, the practical to the pleasurable. Many of these rituals are easy to integrate into the things you already do in everyday life. Rituals help me be. Be present with whatever is coming up and whatever I'm feeling, and just live it without resistance. Be me, fully expressed and fully alive. It is my dearest wish that this book will help you do the same.

There is intentionality behind the order of the rituals in the book. We start with practices that ground you, bring more mindful awareness to your day, and make space for what's to come. Then we move toward deeper practices that expand your intuition, deepen your relationships, and reveal the wisdom hiding within you.

That being said, you can choose to move through this book as you wish. I believe one of the reasons why we've moved away from ritual is because we don't always give ourselves permission to drop the rigidity and put our own spin on the practices. It's your life and you get to make the rules. If you'd like to go through *The Rituals* from cover to cover, go for it. If you'd like to pick the practices that speak to you and focus on those, great. Or you can use the book as an oracle deck and randomly flip open to a ritual each morning to see what the universe has in store. My intention is for you to be guided by whatever feels best for your personal expansion as a spiritual being in this crazy, messy, beautiful, busy human experience.

As you move through this book, I hope you begin to unlock new parts of yourself and discover a grounding peace from which to move through the world and tap into a well of aliveness that lights you up and gives you fuel. I hope you begin to gently transform into your most mindful, attuned, and open self. And I have a gift for you: I've created supplemental materials to support and enhance your practice. You can visit discovertherituals.com for worksheets, guided meditations, and practices designed specifically to enrich your experience of this book.

We are here to connect, to love, to play, to come to know ourselves by knowing each other. So as you move through these pages and experiment with the rituals I've presented, I hope we can begin to build a community around ritual; not just these rituals but ritual as a practice woven into how we live our lives. Say hello on social media by tagging me @nataliemacneil or using the hashtag #therituals as you chronicle your experience or share your own rituals.

We all have gifts to place on the global altar.

Come. Let's dance. The rituals beckon.

—Natalie

DESIGN
YOUR
SACRED
SPACE

———

THIS RITUAL IS PERFECT FOR: Settling into a new home, blessing a space that's just for *you*, reorganizing your office, starting or deepening a spiritual practice.

Humans have cultivated sacred spaces for thousands of years. The oldest temple, Göbekli Tepe in present-day Turkey, dates all the way back to 10,000 B.C.E., a time before humans were making pottery or practicing agriculture. Scientists now hypothesize that it may have been a sacred meeting place for surrounding communities to exchange information, engage in religious ceremony, and feast together. From the temple's vantage point at the top of a hill surrounded by majestic mountains and plains, you can almost imagine these ancient people marveling at the breathtaking view over decadent dishes.

Sacred spaces are often an important part of daily life. In many Southeast Asian countries, the morning starts at small temples, shrines, or altars inside the home or garden. These are spaces where people connect to the divine in a way that feels true for them, where intentions and prayers drip from the heart like sweet nectar, and where offerings are made from the deepest wells of gratitude. The day is embraced through ritual.

Now it's your turn to embrace this tradition by creating a sacred space in your home that honors your beliefs, values, and dreams—a space that roots you in your intention and purpose. There are no set requirements; your sacred space could be a small table, a corner of your bedroom, or even an entire room.

And there are no rules for what goes into it—it's best to listen to your inner voice and let it guide you as you choose meaningful objects and materials for your space. The key is awareness: you don't have to include a statuette or photo just because that's what you've seen on other altars. Instead, pay attention to what resonates with your inner being. And, if one of the things you've chosen ceases to be meaningful, you can simply remove it from your space.

Here are a few ideas to inspire you:

An altar made from a
small table or wooden box

Fresh or dry flowers

Candles or oil burners

Photographs of people you want to honor
(maybe a beloved ancestor)

Objects that speak to you and inspire
the stage of the journey you're on

Statues of goddesses, gods, saints,
or other figures you feel a connection to

Notes from your self-journaling
or personal mantras

Materials that evoke the natural world, like
feathers, rocks and crystals, or leaves

Make this space your own. It will be your sanctuary
and safe haven, a place you can return to whenever
you need to shift your energy, ground yourself, or
be reminded of what's real and true. You may even
do some of the rituals throughout this book in this
sacred space you create.

ANCHOR
YOURSELF

Expressing yourself more fully, deepening self-awareness and connection, working toward a dream or goal, building unshakable confidence.

In the Design Your Sacred Space ritual (page 12), you created a sacred space in your home. In this one, you will connect to your own body as a sacred space. It is the most hallowed place you'll ever dwell in during your human experience.

The jewelry, scents, and clothing we choose to adorn our bodies with have incredible power. You're likely already familiar with the idea of a talisman: an object infused with divine magic that can bring success, protect the wearer or user from evil and harm, or be programmed to serve another purpose. In ancient Greece, a knot talisman symbolized eternal love (that's where the phrase "tying the knot" comes from). The ancient Egyptians kept scarab beetle talismans that symbolized rebirth and the cycles of life. Meaningful objects like this are present in cultures throughout the world.

Today, the way we dress and the accessories, scents, or items we choose speak volumes to the people around us. The way we adorn ourselves is an opportunity for self-expression. It communicates who we are and what we stand for before we even utter a word.

You likely already have a signature adornment of your own—maybe an outfit that you feel confident in, a statement piece of jewelry you often wear, or a go-to scent or oil that makes you feel vibrant. These things aren't just fashion: they anchor you to the deepest parts of yourself, connecting you to your goals, your dreams, and to the core of who you truly are. And, since you are essentially wearing your inner being on the outside, these choices reveal those parts of you to the world.

Adorning yourself and taking care of how your body feels and looks on your own terms is a great way to feel empowered and inspired.

Being fully able to express yourself through your personal style and self-care routine is an exquisite way to spend each day in ritual, reminding yourself, as well as the world, exactly who you are.

Let's begin.

Choose one object as your "anchor." It may be a piece of jewelry, shirt, jacket, plant-based essential oil, or perfume you love. Find a place to sit quietly for a few minutes with the object. Close your eyes, calm your mind, and listen to your breath. Be present in your body. Then, tune in to what you want to embody right now in your life—courage, love, wisdom, creativity, ecstasy, power—whatever feels right to you.

Next, think about a time when you were fully embodying it in the past; for example, a time you felt powerful. Keeping your eyes closed, go back to that time. What are you seeing? What are you feeling? What are you tasting or smelling? Once you feel that tingling sensation of power, touch the object, open your eyes to look at it, and take a few deep breaths.

Finally, focus on a goal or something important that's ahead of you, and allow that vibrant energy you've cultivated to flow from you into the object.

Wear your anchor talisman and see how it changes the way you feel: Do you feel more confident? More aware? You can adorn yourself with your new talisman every day or on special occasions.

MINDFUL
MORNING

THIS RITUAL IS PERFECT FOR: Starting your day powerfully and mindfully, feeling grounded.

Long before Plato invented the first alarm clock in classical Greece (a system of tubes and vessels that filled slowly with water in order to create a loud whistling noise), people were setting intentions for their rise-and-shine hours. Ancient Indian scripts even call the hour and thirty-six minutes before dawn *Brahma muhurta*, the creator's hour.

Morning routines can set the tone for your entire day. I like to spend a few moments each morning visualizing myself in the eye of a hurricane, calm though things around me are chaotic. It centers me before I jump into my day. I will often do a breathing ritual, too, taking long and loud breaths, and rooting myself deep into the earth with each breath. That practice makes me feel I can withstand anything that may come my way.

Having an anchoring morning ritual will help you begin each day equipped and grounded so that you can meet any situation as powerfully as possible. Even when you're confronted with difficulties, you will be able to face that situation with everything you've got and make the best decision for yourself in the moment.

So consider: When you wake up in the morning, how are you starting your day? Are you jumping right into the hurricane? Are you automatically reaching for your phone or computer to review the news and to-do lists and emails? Or are you taking the time to make sure that you are planted in the calm eye of the storm so that you know that you can handle anything that comes your way?

There is no one-size-fits-all morning ritual, and your individual circumstances determine how much time you have before you need to do things like drive to work or get the kids ready for school. You can't take on someone else's routine and hope that it will work exactly the same for you.

The goal of a morning ritual is to provide a space for tuning into yourself and setting an intention before you dive into the world. The rest of it is up to you. You can pull from the rituals throughout this book to create your own morning practice. Here are a few things to keep in mind as you design your own morning ritual:

Do not check your phone first thing in the morning. That immediately takes you out of the calm center of the hurricane. Our phones are amazing tools, but they also drown us in information and must-dos without pause. It's a good idea to set your phone on airplane mode as you go to bed and return it to normal only after your morning ritual is done. Try it!

Hydrate. After not having water for several hours, your body needs it first thing in the morning to boost your metabolism and flush toxins. Keep a big glass of water by your bedside to drink upon waking.

Do something for your body, something for your mind, and something for your spirit. Our bodies need to move, and moving first thing in the morning creates movement and momentum for the day ahead. Put on a song you love and dance, stretch, do squats and pushups, or do any combination of the above. Spend a few minutes meditating and breathing deeply to start the day with a calm mind. There's nothing like writing or speaking aloud the things you're most grateful for. You can do this with other loved ones in your home, too, and build a ritual together.

ALARMING
INSPIRATION

———

THIS RITUAL IS PERFECT FOR: Getting inspired, nourishing yourself throughout the day, staying connected to what matters.

As we move through our day, it's easy to be thrown off track by the competing demands and distractions asking for our attention. From our social media profiles to our text messages and email inboxes, it can feel as if we're being constantly bombarded. This habit of constantly switching among tasks has many different consequences for your brain, but its biggest effect is on your productivity. It can drastically decrease your level of productivity throughout the day as your brain divides its energy and attention among tasks, lowering the quality of attention given to each one.

It's unrealistic to expect to truly cut yourself off from all these distractions. They're a part of our world, whether we like it or not. You do, however, have control over your relationship with them.

In this ritual you will turn this constant barrage of beeps and pings on its head by making it work for you, so you can create more of what you desire most.

Start by setting five inspiration alarms for yourself that go off throughout the day to remind you to stay focused on your intentions, and motivate you with affirmations or mantras to keep going.

Label each of your alarms depending on what you need most. Do you need creative inspiration? Do you need to remind yourself to get up and move around? Do you need to tell yourself to be grateful?

Start there, and space alarms strategically through-out the day.

You can even prerecord short (think thirty seconds) pep talks for yourself that are focused on each particular goal. Then use this recording as your strategic inspiration alarm tone.

When each alarm goes off, take the time to stop and reflect on these messages. They're important, they're from you, and they're just for you. Give them as much time and attention as you'd give an Instagram post from your favorite lifestyle guru or a newsletter detailing your favorite all-natural recipes.

This ritual is designed to bring some control to our world of limitless distraction, and mindfulness to technology designed to take it away from us. It's a way to nourish awareness of our intention and how it correlates to our surroundings.

WALK THROUGH

THE WORLD TODAY

BELIEVING ALL OF

LIFE IS IN LOVE

WITH YOU.

ENCHANTED
EVENING

THIS RITUAL IS PERFECT FOR: Getting good sleep, winding down the day, feeling grounded, nourishing your body.

In many cultures, sleep is considered sacred. Aboriginal Australians believe that the "Dreamtime" contains past, present, and future, as well as the seeds for all creation. Hindu mythology tells the story of the god Vishnu dreaming up the entire Universe, which then flowered out of his navel.

Our bodies have evolved to follow a pattern, the circadian rhythm, that directs when to be active and when to rest. But many of us face the temptation to keep working and be productive into the night, which ultimately disrupts our natural rhythms and exhausts our bodies.

Resting properly is crucial for restoring your brain connections, giving memories a chance to become fixed in your mind, and maintaining your overall health and productivity. Sometimes sleep can help you get more done than doing more work can, as counterintuitive as that may seem.

In this ritual, you're invited to create an evening practice for yourself that feels nourishing and prepares your body for rest. You can pull from the rituals throughout this book to create your own Enchanted Evening. Here are a few things to get you started in designing your evening ritual:

Remove blue light from your environment at least two hours before bed. Blue light from your computer and phone screens suppresses melatonin production. Your phone likely has a setting for night mode, where blue light is removed from the screen after the sun goes down, and you can download a computer app that will remove the blue light from your computer screen in the evening, too. If you watch television at night, you can replace this activity with a more calming practice from this book, like the Tea (or Coffee) Ceremony on page 96. If you still prefer television, buy a pair of blue light–blocking glasses so your brain can prepare for rest.

Clear your mind. As you start to wind down for the evening, you probably still have things from the day running through your mind. Therapeutic journaling is an effective way to let these things go. Sit with the blank page, take three deep breath cycles, and start writing whatever is on your mind. It does not have to be logical. You don't need to solve anything. Simply get everything out. When you are done, place your hand over the page and say aloud, "I release these thoughts, and I am ready for rest."

Connect with loved ones. Root yourself in what matters most, whether that's time at home with your family or calling someone you care about to catch up. There is nothing more important than connecting with the people we share our lives with.

Clean off the day. Release tension by treating yourself to sumptuous self-care. The Cleansing Bath ritual on page 44 is an amazing addition to your Enchanted Evening that will cleanse and purify the body, mind, and soul from energies and situations you encountered throughout the day. After bathing, spray magnesium oil onto your body to help you achieve a deep sleep. It works wonders. Magnesium oil should be rinsed off after about twenty minutes—after you rinse off, you can massage yourself with a lotion before getting into your pajamas.

Disconnect from tech. Before you get in bed, put your phone on airplane mode or leave it outside your bedroom. A transmitting phone next to you at night may impact your sleep.

Sweet dreams, dear one.

DOCUMENT
YOUR
DREAMS

THIS RITUAL IS PERFECT FOR: Deepening your spiritual practice, connecting to your inner wisdom, exploring your mind.

When you wake up, there's usually a very small window in which you can recall your dreams in vivid detail. Then, they dissipate from your memory. For this ritual you'll keep a small journal or notepad by your bed, or somewhere obvious enough that you'll remember to pick it up every morning.

While many people laugh dreams off as the brain's weird, late-night musings, dreams can hold an incredible amount of wisdom and truth for our daily lives if we're willing to dial in and really pay attention.

Native American and Aboriginal cultures see dreams as critically important, and base many important decisions for their societies on their dreams. Ancient Greeks, as documented in *The Odyssey*, thought of some dreams as visitations from deities, come to give instructions, healing, or dire warnings. It's safe to say that they took the content of these dreams very seriously.

Renowned psychologist Carl Jung thought of dreams as portals that let us access an incredibly wise, collective, and unconscious mind, shared with all of humankind, that we can't reach in waking life.

In short, listening to dream messages can unlock endless lessons about where you are in life, where you're headed, and how you can align with your innermost guide.

Let's start your dream journal.

Upon waking, grab your pen and journal immediately. If you had a dream, write down anything you can recall, even if it seems silly. Were there colors? Were there plot details? What people were there? Where were you?

Try to think about any objects you saw, any feelings you felt, words that you heard, or conversations that you had. Just write away! Nothing constrains you: jot it down as bullet points, long paragraphs, out of order, or even as a comic strip if you want. It doesn't need to be a masterpiece of a story. It's about noticing the key details.

If you're curious, you can look up the meanings in a dream or symbol dictionary online.

Review this journal when you're making big decisions or working toward new goals. Notice how your dreams align with what's going on in your life. Your journal might just contain the wise guidance you are seeking.

If you don't remember your dreams, you can still add to this journal. The moments after you wake

up are the perfect time for a stream of consciousness writing practice. Here's how it works:

Take a few deep breaths and ask for guidance or
divine inspiration to pour forth through you.

Open your eyes and begin writing what comes
through without thinking about it or worrying
about punctuation or spelling.

Don't take your pen off the paper until you feel the
download is complete.

FLAME-GAZING MEDITATION

———

THIS RITUAL IS PERFECT FOR: Meditation, improving the health of your eyes, releasing the stress of the day, improving concentration, counteracting the impact of blue light.

Trāṭaka, meaning "to gaze" in Sanskrit, is a yogic technique of gazing at a flame believed to activate increased powers of focus and memory. This technique is thought to cleanse not just the eyes, but also your energy field, filling you with a deep sense of clarity and peace. Master practitioners say that if you spend enough time focusing on the flame, it will cast new light on situations or conflicts unfolding in your life, too.

This ritual is essential for anyone who spends a lot of time looking at screens. Practice this regularly to release stress on your eyes (and even if your screen time is minimal, this practice has many benefits).

When you're staring at a screen all day, you're blinking half as much as usual, which can lead to dryness, blurry vision, irritation, and eye strain. It's important to let your eyes rest after a long day to maintain their long-term health.

Find a quiet, dark space in your home where you can meditate and simply be. Bring a favorite candle with you and find a comfortable place to sit on the floor, using a yoga mat or a meditation cushion. For added benefit, use a candle infused with a calming scent like lavender.

Place the candle at eye level about a foot in front of you. You can measure it by the distance from your elbow to the tips of your fingers.

Light the candle and, in the silence and shadows of the room, concentrate on the way your body starts to relax. Take the deepest breath you have taken all day. Consider setting a simple intention (for example: "I choose love") or lighting the candle in honor of someone.

Focus on the flame, and watch it burn and flicker. Try not to blink.

Hold your gaze until tears fill your eyes. At this point in the practice, vocalize anything you want to release before you move on with your day, or say an affirmation like "I release all the stress, worry, tension, and fear I have been holding on to." When the ritual feels complete to you, blow out the candle.

LET YOUR

LIGHT PERMEATE

THE EDGES OF

YOUR FEARS.

COMMUNE
WITH
THE
COSMOS

———

THIS RITUAL IS PERFECT FOR: Unwinding after a hectic day, unplugging from screens, putting things in perspective, contemplation on next steps.

For as long as humans have walked the earth, we've looked upon the starry night sky with wonder and curiosity: *Why are we here? What does this mean? How did it come to be?* Our fascination with the endless mysteries of the universe might explain why astronomy is one of the oldest natural sciences.

In ancient Babylon, astronomers believed the skies were the home of the gods and goddesses. That's why they tracked the movement of the stars in incredible detail, using them to interpret signs from the divine. The ancient Egyptians positioned their greatest architectural feats and monuments in alignment with the stars; the Great Pyramid of Giza aligns with the North Star. And some historians believe that Portugal's ancient "passage graves"—elongated corridors built into the earth—were designed to offer complete darkness for a clear view of the stars six thousand years before the first telescope.

Perhaps our wonder at those far-away twinkling lights and planets above us stems from our own origins.

Medieval philosophers spoke of the macrocosm (the universe) and the microcosm (the body and soul) as reflections of each other. Mirroring the infinite cosmos, our existence is rich, alive, and ever-expanding.

As Carl Sagan said in his 1980 series *Cosmos*, "The cosmos is also within us. We're made of star stuff. We are a way for the cosmos to know itself."

We are a way for the universe, the creator, the cosmos to know itself.

Take that in.

Gazing up at the stars is one of the best antidotes to stress, uncertainty, and that hard-to-shake feeling that the weight of the world is on your shoulders. This process of zooming out helps you gain perspective on your daily challenges and how they fit within the grander scheme of things. As you stare up at the moon, the stars, and the planets circling above you as points of light, you get back in touch with the eternal dance of all that is.

This simple but powerful ritual reminds us we are whole beings within a much larger whole. It roots us in the remembrance of that cosmic origin.

Let's begin.

You can do this alone or with your loved ones, but make sure there's nothing to distract you (leave your phone at home or turn it off and tuck it away).

Sit outside on a dark, cloudless night with your favorite hot drink and a blanket, and gaze up at the starry sky (if you don't have access to outdoor space, turn the lights off in your home and sit near an open window with a view of the sky). Give your eyes a few minutes to adjust to the darkness, allowing you to see more stars. The longer you stay, the more you'll see.

See how it feels. Contemplate how you are presently living your life. Take a few moments to think about the things that are causing you stress or uncertainty. Are the situations you perceive as problems really that big in the grand scheme of things?

Think of the future generations that will look up at this same sky. They may even get to visit another planet. There is more space for possibility and for creating beauty than we think. We are alive and get to experience this. Stay with that feeling. Let it flow through you.

CLEANSING
BATH

THIS RITUAL IS PERFECT FOR: Boosting creativity, spiritual cleansing, releasing the day, reducing stress, self-care.

This bathing ritual will cleanse away the day and help you wash away the stress, fears, and energy you take on from the people and spaces around you (not to mention the sweat and dirt you pick up from just being in the world).

Water rituals are some of the most beautiful, cleansing experiences we can offer ourselves. They have been practiced for centuries across cultures— from Turkish and Moroccan *hamams*, to Russian *banyas*, to Korean *jjimjilbangs*, to Japanese *onsen* bathhouses—and many are still practiced today.

You don't need a bathhouse in order to enjoy your very own water ritual. For this bathing practice, you just need a bathtub, a washcloth or loofah, and a few simple ingredients:

> 2 cups [550 g] rock salt (for the magnesium and minerals your body needs)
>
> ¼ cup [60 ml] apple cider vinegar
>
> 2 or 3 tablespoons coconut oil
>
> 5 to 10 drops rose, lavender, or other favorite essential oil
>
> Flower petals (your choice—romance yourself!)

Run yourself a bath and mix the ingredients together in the warm water of the tub. Immerse yourself in the water and, using a washcloth or loofah, begin to wash every inch of yourself. Cherish your body—do this very slowly. As you move your washcloth in circles, visualize yourself detaching everything negative or stressful from your body and releasing it into the nourishing water. Be as sensual as you wish when you pamper yourself: Try running the rose petals over your skin and slowly washing your hair from the crown to the ends. Take your time. Indulge yourself.

When you're finished, step out of the bath, unplug the drain, and declare: "And I let it all go."

For those who prefer a shower over a bath, or don't have access to a bathtub, this ritual can be adapted for the shower, too. Showering is often a core part of our daily routine—so why not turn it into a simple ritual to start or end the day?

As you step into the shower, visualize the water turning into white light that clears negative energy away from your skin and inner being.

Combining a handful of sea salt and spoonful of coconut oil, scrub your body and visualize scrubbing away anything that's been bothering you. The salt and the water are symbols of purification. You can add a couple drops of your favorite essential oil to the scrub, too.

Bonus points if you do this ritual in a cold shower, as cold water offers an extra energy boost by raising your heart rate, boosting your metabolism, and increasing serotonin levels.

As you rinse the last of the salt scrub away, watch the water drain and declare: "I let it all go, it is not mine to carry anymore."

This transformative ritual turns a mundane daily task into a transformative cleansing practice.

PLANT
YOUR
DREAMS

THIS RITUAL IS PERFECT FOR: Setting goals, reminding yourself of your own progress, staying connected to your growth.

Seeds are magical. They're like tiny factories, designed to contain absolutely everything they need to become a fruit, vegetable, flower, bush—even the tallest, most majestic tree.

After a seed is planted and watered, it reaches a tendril into the darkness of the earth. There in the quiet blackness of the soil, a shoot will begin to expand upward toward the light and break the ground. Slowly, the plant begins its journey into its fullest expression: up, up, and up until it's a being that blooms, drops its fruit, or reaches its branches up to the heavens. This is the miracle: a full life is contained in one tiny, little seed. Many mythologies, from Vedism in ancient India to traditional Polynesian beliefs, involve the story of one primordial seed giving birth to the entire complex universe.

Planting a seed is the perfect metaphor for manifesting the goals and dreams you're working toward. You've probably heard the saying "Plant the seed" in reference to an idea designed to grow into something else. Well, what if we took that literally?

Next time you start working toward a new dream—whether it's landing a promotion at work, launching a new business, or saving up for a trip you've been longing to take—plant a seed at the same time. There's a deep beauty in nurturing life, and even more in nurturing a plant while you're also working toward a goal. It's powerful work—putting all of your intentions into a seed, planting it, and taking care of it while it sends down roots, breaks through the soil, and grows toward the light. There's something delightful about that process, and it keeps you rooted in your goals and your intentions. You are nourishing not just another living thing, but also yourself at the same time. Remember that just like the seed, you have everything within you to make your dream happen.

Be patient. The growing plant is a marvelous reminder that your deepest, grandest desires and goals take time to flourish, bloom, and bear fruit. It can take an apple tree years to produce a single apple.

What happens when the goal is reached or the plant is fully grown? You keep nurturing your plant. It will be a precious reminder of the journey you've traveled. Keep it in your home or in your sacred space, to remind you that you are strong, resilient, and capable of great things.

A SEED CONTAINS
EVERYTHING IT NEEDS
TO GROW THROUGH
THE DARKNESS AND
TOWARD THE LIGHT
TO EXPAND INTO ITS
FULLEST POTENTIAL.
AND SO DO YOU.

YOUR
HOLY
DAY

THIS RITUAL IS PERFECT FOR: Staying present, relaxing your mind and body, recharging your energy for the week ahead.

The world's major religions have a holy day each week. The Jewish Sabbath begins just before sunset on Friday evenings. The Sabbath is a day of rest that reminds followers of the day of rest God took after creating the earth. Christians worship and rest on Sundays in the tradition of the community apostolic church. In Islam, Fridays are spent observing Jumu'ah, a day for worship and togetherness.

In these religious traditions, holy days provide a break from the rushing of everyday life. It's a time to be with loved ones and to worship without anything else demanding your attention—a day to just be one with the deity.

In this ritual, you will reserve one day a week for no work. This day is about connection, joy, nature, art.

In today's fast-paced world, it can feel difficult—or even seem indulgent—to take one day completely off, unplugged from your work, your inbox, your obligations, and your to-do list. But taking time away can actually help you feel more creative, alert, and energized.

Start your holy day ritual by picking out one day of the week where you can completely unplug from your work and emails. Once you've picked out your day, schedule it in your calendar as a recurring event, and treat it as an essential appointment that you can't cancel.

Having an unscheduled day might seem over-whelming at first. If you're unsure of what to do with your day off, take out a pen and some paper and write down some activities or places you visited recently that made you feel completely present and relaxed. This could be anything from your favorite yoga class to family time to simply reading a book without any distractions.

Here are some ideas for activities that can help you stay grounded and present on your holy day:

Taking a long walk in nature

Exercising

Gardening

Cooking a healthy meal

Being out in the sunshine

Taking a long Epsom salt bath

Spending time with loved ones

Writing handwritten letters
to friends and family

Journaling

Drawing or painting

Reflecting the past week and any
emotions, triggers, dominating thoughts,
or milestones that emerged

Doing absolutely nothing at all
(easier said than done)

The important thing about your holy day is to be strict about keeping it free of work and digital distractions. This can be a difficult adjustment if you're someone who always feels the need to be connected. However, ask yourself, "Will my career, business, or job completely fail if I take one day a week to myself?" Of course it won't! Our mind loves to play tricks on us by creating problems that are not only not there but are also quite irrational once we take a step back and truly think about them.

RELEASE
AND
RISE

———

THIS RITUAL IS PERFECT FOR: Releasing the past, creating space for the new, forgiveness, healing.

In mythical tales from ancient Arabia and Egypt, it was said that an eagle-like bird with deep red and gold plumage lived to be hundreds of years old, and could be seen soaring across the sprawling desert landscape of Arabia. Toward the end of its life, it would spread its wings and fly to Heliopolis, the Egyptian "City of the Sun."

There, perched on the highest peak of the Temple of the Sun, the old bird would make a nest of fragrant cinnamon twigs and resin, and wait. As the sun crept over the horizon, the bird would let out a sharp cry. As soon as the golden rays hit the top of the temple, the old bird would burst into flames, creating a pillar of smoke, dense black against the desert sky.

Once the fire was out and the ashes had gone cold, a new, tiny body emerged from these ashes—ready to soar through another cycle in all its fiery magnificence. The phoenix from Greek mythology goes through this kind of cyclical transformation, too.

In this ritual, I invite you to go through your own rebirth in the form of a fire ceremony and allow what you no longer want in your life to go up in smoke. This ritual is a beautiful way to release what you want to let go of and step onto a clear slate, a fresh cycle of your life.

To begin your fire ritual, first decide what you'd like to release and burn away.

It might be a belief about yourself you wish to release. Or a person you've had a difficult relationship with. Or a project or goal that you've completed and want to let go of so you can move on to the next big thing. Whatever it is, write it down on a small piece of paper.

Next, write down something that belief, relationship, or situation gave you. What did you learn? In which way did you grow? Even from patterns and situations that are painful, great lessons and strength can arise. How can you share those lessons and gifts with the world? That's how we all contribute to transformation and evolution.

Then, find a space where burning paper is safe—an outdoor fire pit, a fireplace, or even a tin can in your backyard. Put on some of your favorite music and light some incense, or just stand in the silence.

Set your paper aflame. Watch the embers fly and the ashes float, taking with it your fears, your pain, your goals, and your hopes for the next leg of your journey. Accept whatever that may be without judgment. Your journey is your own, and no one but yourself can give you peace.

Stay a while as the fire burns out and spend time reflecting on the lessons of that particular cycle of your life. Bask in the moment; relish the release.

YOUR DIVINE
CREATIVE IMPULSE
WILL OFTEN CALL
ON YOU TO DESTROY
BEFORE YOU CREATE.
DESTRUCTION FIRST,
THEN THE DESIRED
OUTCOME.

HONOR
YOUR
ANCESTORS

———

THIS RITUAL IS PERFECT FOR: Memorializing loved ones, revisiting your family lineage, anchoring to the truth of who you are, strengthening your ties to yourself and previous generations who laid the path for you.

We stand on the shoulders of those who came before us, just as future generations will stand upon ours. Our great-grandparents could never have imagined the life we live now, lit by advanced technology and surrounded by social, economic, and cultural circumstances so different than their own. In this ritual, we honor those who came before and feel their presence within us, and we recognize that we, ourselves, will become the ancestors of future generations.

In the traditional beliefs of cultures from the ancient Scandinavians to the current residents of Madagascar, the dead are still part of the human community, and they still have great importance: as deciders of fate, givers of wisdom, or simply the force that binds us together.

When we choose to honor those who have passed on, and all that their actions have created for us, our souls reach across time and space to touch theirs as we remember who we are. We become alive in a deeper way.

NOTE: *For some people, reflecting on your ancestry may bring up pain, anger, or trauma. If this ritual is triggering to you, please stop and get support from a group or practitioner that specializes in ancestral trauma.*

There are a few ways you can practice this ritual:

Uncover your ancestry. If you are not yet familiar with your ancestry, consider discovering your roots through a simple DNA test. These companies use cutting-edge DNA splicing technology to help you move through each of your twenty-three pairs of chromosomes and discover the ancestral magic that is within your cells.

The awareness of where and who you come from is a beautiful way to celebrate how you came to exist here. If you are descended from settlers, this is even more important, as you might experience a feeling of drifting and not-belonging. Finding the land and the people who gave birth to you is crucial to finding your own magic, your own sense of identity. You are more than what our system wants you to be: you are the most important legacy of everyone who came before you.

Create an altar to your ancestors. Add photos, objects, or anything else that represents your lineage to the sacred space you've created in your home. Reflect on your ancestors—perhaps imagine what their lives might have been like, what clothes they wore, what their home might have looked like, what traditions they practiced. Place beautiful flowers and candles on the altar to honor them, or any adornments you see fit.

Correspond with those who came before you. Write a letter to those in your lineage, either to specific groups of people or to individuals, like a great-grandparent. These letters can offer gratitude, express pain, ask for a piece of wisdom, share what you're most proud of about your culture and ancestry, or express whatever else is in your heart. Burn the letter after you write it.

Cook a traditional dish from the country your ancestors came from. In Hindu tradition, food, taste, and smell are related to the root chakra (center of energy), or *Muladhara*. Making a meal your ancestors might have also eaten connects you with them in a very direct way.

AUGURY
DAY

———

THIS RITUAL IS PERFECT FOR: Setting the tone for a new phase in your life, honing your intuition, connecting with your future self.

Augury, the ancient practice of using omens to decipher the will of the gods, goes back thousands of years and was practiced in ancient civilizations in Europe, China, and Egypt.

Omens are signs from the external world that can be used to predict the future. For example, in ancient Rome augurs would observe weather patterns and birds to make predictions of what was to come.

The ritual presented here is a contemporary interpretation I've done with my dear friend Layla Martin, rooted in the ancient tradition. Instead of trying to decipher the flights of birds or the weather, I invite you to seek omens everywhere and create ones for yourself.

Augury Day is a day when you set intentions for the next cycle of your life and fully embody those intentions. It should be celebrated on the cusp of a new beginning—the first day of the year, a birthday, or the first day of the month or lunar cycle.

As you plan your own Augury Day, write down the energies, essences, and feelings you want to embody during this new cycle. Looking at those words, what activities and experiences can you build into your Augury Day that are in alignment with your goals?

For example, if you're setting a goal to be healthier and more connected to nature in the New Year, on January 1 you could plan an Augury Day where you eat healthy and nourishing food and take an adventure through the woods. Or, if you want to bring creativity into the month ahead, spend the first day of the month painting or working on a collage. Do whatever makes you feel like you're embodying the essences, energies, and intention in the words you wrote.

Planning isn't everything, though. Throughout your Augury Day, remain open. Is there a word or phrase or number you keep seeing? Are you stumbling across a favorite flower or animal you connect with? Do you receive a phone call or email, or have an unexpected event change the course of your day? Pay attention to signs you come across as the day unfolds, as well as in your dreams, and write those down.

Do your plans seem wild, extreme, full, or restful? As you live out your Augury Day, note the moments that light you up, any signs you come across, or things that feel meaningful. Bring those feelings and experiences into the new cycle you're entering.

YOUR SOUL
REMEMBERS
TRUTHS
YOUR MIND
CANNOT.

WRITE
YOUR
OBITUARY

———

THIS RITUAL IS PERFECT FOR: Reflecting on your life—past and present, self-exploration, uncovering what you desire to change.

Death is an unavoidable part of life. Yet in Western culture, most of us don't confront death until it's right in front of us, such as when a loved one passes or we come face-to-face with our own mortality in a near-death experience. It may sound dark, but there is freedom and aliveness in reflecting on death and confronting your own death head-on. Our impermanence does not have to frighten us. It is an opportunity to explore everything we want to do while living.

In some parts of the world, death is seen as a holy transition into what comes after. In Bali, Indonesia, for example, funeral rites can require the participation of entire villages and take days or even weeks to carry out, ending in a sumptuous celebratory feast that frees the person's soul so it can begin its next life. In Mexico, the holiday Día de Muertos (Day of the Dead) honors those who have passed on through prayer, ritual, food and other offerings.

Being conscious of death can make life's precious, small moments—like a conversation with a loved one, the colors of a sunset—more significant. Bhutanese religious practice tells us to reflect on our own death five times a day. This is not meant to make us feel fearful; rather, it should help you appreciate your day and move through it with deeper awareness.

Obituaries commemorate a life and everything that person touched, loved, and created in this physical world. But it is difficult to sum up someone's entire existence within a short piece of writing. It's like trying to fit an ocean into a teacup! However, it can also be a powerful exercise in memory, connection, love, and dedication. Obituaries reveal what was most important about an individual and what comes through when considering their deepest essence. By thinking about what matters most about someone at the very end, you can gain enormous amounts of clarity and appreciation for their existence.

I want you to experience that for yourself.

In this ritual, you will write your own obituary.

Sit in a quiet space. Breathe deeply. Visualize taking your last breaths in this body. Reflect on your life. How do you think you'll be remembered? How do you want to be remembered? Make sure your writing reflects not just what you've accomplished (professional goals, for example), but also your deeper purpose and the truth of who you are. It should speak to the way you expressed yourself in the world and what gifts you left behind: your inheritance for future generations.

Journal until you feel your obituary captures
who you really are and who you'd like to be. It's
a powerful exercise, and I invite you to see what
comes up.

Reading your obituary, what changes can you make
to be in alignment with the life you want to live and
the legacy you want to leave?

What truly matters in terms of reaching the core
of who you are and what you want to be? How do
your daily actions all contribute to that?

WELCOME
THE
NEW
SEASON

THIS RITUAL IS PERFECT FOR: Embracing change, connecting to the ancient practice of ushering in a new season in ritual.

The changing of the seasons has long been a reason for celebration and observance in cultures around the world. England's famous Stonehenge was likely a temple (or, at the very least, a very majestic tool) to observe and celebrate equinoxes, solstices, and solar eclipses.

In Japan, Shunbun no Hi, also known as Vernal Equinox Day, is a national holiday, as well as a time for children to head home to spend time with their families and honor the lives and graves of their ancestors.

Hindus celebrate spring with the "festival of colors" known as Holi. They dance through the streets and play while showering each other with powders in every joyful shade of the rainbow.

The Iranian New Year of Nowruz, on the spring equinox, is a tradition dating back thousands of years. It is celebrated with two weeks of time spent with loved ones, swapping gifts, gathering, and feasting around bonfires.

When we take time to acknowledge the changing of the seasons, we are also taking time to acknowledge our own shifts and life cycles. We are not the same day to day, week to week, or month to month. This ritual gives you a chance to reflect on this.

As you transition from one season to the next, take time to reflect on where you've been and where you hope to go. As season changes—the summer and winter solstices and the spring and fall equinoxes—start paying more attention to the natural world around you, and allow it to spark your own personal inquiry. Are plants blooming and growing? What is blooming and growing in your life? What is wilting and dying? Are there any aspects of your life that are waning? Feel the changing patterns and how they affect not only the natural life, but also you.

Celebrate who you were in the last few months and embrace expanding into your highest self with the changing of the season. These are some questions and prompts to reflect on as part of this practice:

This season of life brought…
The lessons this season taught me were…
What aspects of myself were revealed in these three months?
What parts of myself am I still hiding in the shadows?
In this next season and cycle I'm ready for…

Create time and space to be in nature at this time. This can mean an action as simple as taking a walk in the park to see the changing leaves or watching the sunset through your window.

Our ancestors welcomed new seasons with group celebrations. So, bonus points for you if you cocreate this ritual with a loved one or a group of friends.

UPSIDE-DOWN DAY

———

THIS RITUAL IS PERFECT FOR: Perspective shifts, exploring new parts of your being, letting go of control and flowing with life.

Inversion rituals—rituals that turn social norms on their head—remind revelers of the fragility of social conventions and of the shared, common humanity of everyone: what really lies underneath crowns, armor, politics, and titles. In many cultures around the world, rituals of inversion are carried out to great celebration.

For example, Brazil's lavish Carnival festival is a way to "invert" society just before the restrictive season of Lent begins. People dress in elaborate costumes and indulge in food and drink—the opposite way of life while observing Lent.

The ancient Celts celebrated a more metaphysical kind of inversion ritual: Samhain (the inspiration for modern-day Halloween). On this day, it was believed, the spirits of the dead and the gods came to the human world and acted as living people. So, in order to avoid meeting them, the actual living wore masks that looked like the faces of the dead. The point was to turn the world upside down, confuse, and play, all the while having a good feast with family and community.

In a tarot deck, the Hanged Man card shows a man hung from a tree by his foot, his head close to the ground. The name and the imagery of this card can, at first, seem scary—just as inversions can seem scary—but its message is one of renovation. In order to grow spiritually and creatively, the Hanged Man suggests, you need to shake things up. You need to get a radically fresh perspective.

Inversions allow us to rebel against the routines that dictate much of our world. The fresh perspective that comes from a flipped routine, exploring a new route home, or taking an impromptu nap in the middle of the day is incredibly powerful. These small acts of switching up the norm might seem trivial, but their effect can trickle down into all areas of your life.

Practicing inversion is like exercise for your brain—it swiftly adjusts to the change and creates new pathways that open doors to entirely new ways of thinking. You are sparking a fresh start for your creative, productive, and inventive spirit.

Ready to try this perspective shifting ritual? I invite you to get playful with this ritual. Let's invert.

Inversions do not have to be extreme. Here are some ideas:

Write or eat using your nondominant hand.

Have breakfast for dinner.

Take a new route to work.

Wear your partner or best friend's clothes.

Sleep with your head where your feet usually are.

Read a favorite poem from last line to first line.

If none of these ideas appeal to you, you might prefer a different approach: remain open to impulse. If you're walking along the street and something catches your eye around the corner, take the turn! If you see someone reading an interesting book during your commute, ask them about it. The possibilities are endless. The key is to spark inspiration and remain open to people, opportunities, and experiences that you might otherwise not notice in your day-to-day routine.

EMBRACE
IMPERFECTION

THIS RITUAL IS PERFECT FOR: Deepening your love (for your partner, friends, family, and yourself), celebrating and accepting what is.

We are all perfectly imperfect. Accepting that fact about ourselves and others can eliminate a lot of frustration and save a lot of energy. This ritual invites you to see beauty in imperfection and deliberately seek out reasons to embrace and adore what you perceive as flaws in yourself and those around you.

This practice is embodied in the Japanese tradition of *wabi-sabi*. While there's no direct translation from Japanese to English, essentially it refers to the practice of appreciating authenticity rather than perfection. It's the belief that there's beauty in a chipped vase, a cloudy December landscape, aged wood, or a rusted piece of metal. It's the practice of looking at something that seems, at first, ugly or dismissible and finding its beauty.

When it comes to your relationship with yourself and others, it's important to recognize flaws as expressions of our existence as human beings. Recognizing this, and practicing how to appreciate authenticity, can open new doors for connection, appreciation, and love.

When someone close to you does something that doesn't meet an expectation you had or triggers you, take a moment before you react and ask yourself, "Is reacting to this really worth my time and energy right now? How will I feel after reacting, and how would I feel instead if I chose to accept this?"

Find three things you love and appreciate about that person—three things about them that make you happy—and hold these in your mind as you take a few breaths. Extend this love to them in your heart and then, and only then, act and share from a loving place what's coming up for you.

You can introduce this concept to your perception of yourself, to what you see in the mirror: Embrace your imperfections. They are beautiful, too. In our heavily Photoshopped and social media–edited culture, embracing imperfection can be a revolutionary practice of radical self-love.

Begin by standing in front of a mirror. What do you see? Hold yourself authentically; don't pose. You are witnessing the beauty of your own being.

Look into your own eyes and hold your gaze. Focus on breathing deeply. After you've taken eight deep inhalations and exhalations, take your gaze to the rest of your body. Pause in the areas you find difficult to accept. Perhaps it's your scars, your freckles, your belly, your arms, a facial feature—we all have our little insecurities.

Now, instead of judging what you see, flip the script: Say, "I love that perfectly imperfect part of me" and "I appreciate my journey." Place your hands on whatever part of your body you are focusing on and find something to love and be grateful for about that part of you.

MINDFUL
EATING

THIS RITUAL IS PERFECT FOR: Developing a beautiful relationship with food, bonding with loved ones around food, improving health, feeling good in your body.

Food is essential for all of us. Because food is crucial to our survival, many cultures have developed inspiring practices, customs, and rituals around meals.

The ancient Bedouin groups that inhabit the harsh Middle Eastern deserts share food with anyone passing through. Traditionally, any traveler that arrives at a Bedouin settlement has the right to shelter and a meal. In turn, guests agree to respect their hosts. This dynamic fosters cooperation among strangers and became the foundation for life-changing relationships.

Sobremesa in Central and South American cultures literally means "over the table" and refers to the time following the main course of the meal. Everyone at the table relaxes, eats sweets, drinks coffee or traditional liquors, and connects with the other guests. People tell funny stories, share memories, and revel in each other's company.

Food rituals are less common in Western societies. Many people consume food mindlessly, and this detachment from the action of eating is linked to a myriad of health issues. Developing a practice of *mindful* eating can help us improve our health, eat better in terms of quality and quantity, and bond with our friends and family.

I want to invite you to form your own ritual for mindful eating. This ritual will help you shift your approach to one that honors the food you consume, the world that made it, and your own being. This ritual will look different for everyone, as we have diverse eating settings and practices.

Here are some tips to get started:

When you're deciding what to eat, check in with your body. Feel what it needs and tune in to what will most benefit you in this moment.

If you're making the food yourself, before you begin preparing the meal, take thirty seconds to visualize pouring love and gratitude from your heartspace into the food.

If someone else prepared the food, place your hands over the food and take thirty seconds to give gratitude for the food that is about to nourish your body. Think about where it came from, how much work was involved in getting it to you, and who was involved in preparing it. You can say a little prayer over the food or simply say, "Thank you for this nourishment."

If possible, enjoy your meal at a table. Give your attention to the food in front of you and the people you're sharing it with, or your own thoughts if you're eating alone. Avoid watching TV or scrolling through your phone while you eat.

As you eat, chew slowly. Notice the flavors and textures. Savor each bite you take. Eating slowly can improve digestion.

After you've finished eating, give yourself at least twenty minutes at the table without the pressure of being productive. This is the time for *sobremesa*. Share a good conversation with those you're eating with while allowing your body to settle. If you're alone, this is a great time for journaling or reading. Once you've finished, repeat, "Thank you for this nourishment," before proceeding with the rest of your day.

THE
GAME
OF
GRATITUDE

—————

Shifting into a state of joy and appreciation, beaming out love in every direction, connecting with yourself and your loved ones.

I am so grateful you have this book in your hands.

I am so grateful you're alive and well enough to be able to read and explore these rituals.

I am so grateful you and I are connected as we lean together into a new way of doing and being.

This is the game of gratitude.

Gratitude itself has been shown to improve physical and psychological health, deepen relationships, increase mental strength, and even help you sleep better. Which makes me wonder why we don't approach gratitude like going to the gym, practicing just a little every day to grow stronger, happier, and a little lighter.

The good news is you can do this. Enter the Game of Gratitude.

There are three ways to play this game.

Stream of gratitude. The first way to play is by jumping into a stream of gratitude. To do this, name every single thing you can think of that you are grateful for out loud. Small things, big things, and everything in between. Keep going until you can't think of anything else. This practice will submerge you in a full-on grateful, joyful, vibrant state.

Make a list. The second way to play is to write out a list of ten things you're grateful for in the moment. They don't even have to be big things!

A beautiful ray of sunshine counts, as does a fluffy pillow or a delicious cup of tea. You can do this as part of a ritual in the morning or evening to start or close your day from a place of gratitude.

Ten minutes of gratitude. The third way to play this game is to sit with somebody you love and set a timer for ten minutes. For the first five minutes, you express what you're grateful for in your own life and in your relationship with the other person, while they listen. Then, switch roles! Share your deepest truth, even if it feels a little vulnerable and tender. What do you love about this person who is sitting in front of you right now? What do you see in them that they might not see in themselves? How do they show up in your life? Try to reflect back to them all the beautiful things that you love about them.

The beauty of this ritual is that it doesn't require anything new for you to feel appreciative, satisfied, and fulfilled. All you need to do is tap into the beautiful gifts you already have.

DON'T EXPECT
MORE THAN WHAT
YOU EXPRESS
GRATITUDE
FOR NOW.

FLOW

OF

ABUNDANCE

——

THIS RITUAL IS PERFECT FOR: Being more mindful of spending, feeling abundant, shifting your mind-set around money.

If I ask you to imagine an "abundant lifestyle," your mind may go to someone who flies first class around the world, gets regular massages and pampering, and buys whatever they want without having to consider their budget. Some or all of these things may be part of what abundance looks like to you, and that's okay. But true abundance is about so much more. Living an abundant lifestyle is about cultivating a healthy relationship with money, deeply respecting money everywhere you meet it, appreciating the money that comes into your life, and being comfortable parting with it in order to invest in experiences and things that will bring you joy. The intention of this ritual is to help you tap into a flow of abundance.

Here are a few money rituals that will help you cultivate an abundant lifestyle:

Write your affirmations. Think about how you feel about money and the kind of energy you put out and take in when you're exchanging money. Write three affirmations that envision a better, healthier relationship with money. You can keep the piece of paper on your altar or in a piggy bank.

Practice gratitude. When you're paying a bill, practice gratitude for what it has provided in your life. For example, that monthly phone bill helps you keep in close contact with family and friends who live thousands of miles away.

Manifest ever-flowing abundance. When you find a coin or dollar bill, respect it by picking it up and keeping it somewhere that reminds you of ever-flowing abundance in your life, like a small dish, jar, or even a handmade piggy bank. Though you may think finding something as small as a penny doesn't mean anything, it's a reminder from the universe that money—and abundance—is everywhere.

Donate your coins. Place a bowl on your altar where you can collect extra or found coins. Once the bowl gets full, donate the funds to a local charity or buy a meal for someone in need. Witness the power of noticing the small things and collecting for the greater good.

Clean out your wallet. Cleaning out your wallet is another way to demonstrate your respect for your money and the healthy value you place on it. Spend some time ridding your wallet of any old receipts and cards you no longer use or need. Put your dollar bills in order. Your wallet is effectively the home for your cash and the debit or credit cards you use every day. Treat it as a home.

Keep a wallet charm. You can also place a small charm or note in your wallet. Pick something that reminds you that your needs will always be met. It can be a small crystal or gemstone that you feel drawn to (jade is a good choice, as it's considered to bring prosperity and luck in many cultures) or anything else that holds significance for you.

TEA (OR COFFEE)
CEREMONY

———

THIS RITUAL IS PERFECT FOR: Warming your heart and your body, setting intentions, practicing mindfulness.

Rituals have the magical ability to turn normal, everyday occurrences into sacred art.

The Chinese tea ceremony is an ancient and fascinating tradition, traditionally called Cha Dao, or the Dao of Tea. This ceremony awakens a deep understanding of the holiness of commonplace things. I encourage you to look up or attend a traditional Chinese ceremony to experience the richness of this cultural experience.

While many of us may enjoy tea by boiling water, plunking a tea bag into a cup, and adding a bit of honey or milk, Chinese ceremonies are so much more involved. Cha Dao can take hours and includes a number of traditional utensils and fixed steps, from the first moment the tea pourer sits down to prepare the beverage for their guest all the way to the final sip.

At the core of these complex tea ceremonies is a fairly simple idea: creating a moment of connection and appreciation—for the tea, the company, and the present experience.

The following ritual is designed to help you inhabit the present moment with a heightened awareness. It aims to encourage you to experience just how beautiful life is, and how sacred. This simple ceremony will bring incredible grounding and fullness into a commonplace daily ritual.

Let's begin.

You will need tea leaves, an infuser, hot water, and a teacup. Bonus points if you designate a teacup specifically for this ceremony, as it will heighten the uniqueness of experience. Make sure you have these items, as well as any extras, such as honey, close at hand.

Set out your items on the table. Appreciate them. Perceive their colors and textures. You are dropping into a state of mindfulness. Breathe.

Prepare your tea. Place some tea leaves in the infuser; not too tight—give them space to breathe.

Heat the water to the right temperature for your leaves (for example, for green tea, the water should be just short of boiling) and pour it over the infuser.

Hold the cup in your hands. Warmth irradiates from it just as it does from you; you're both beacons of light and aliveness in the universe.

Stay present in the process. Infuse the beverage with your intentions: What do you want to take in?

How can you offer more warmth and comfort—
both to others and yourself—in your daily life?
Pour your hopes, dreams, and wishes into the cup.

When the tea is at your preferred intensity and temperature, take out the infuser. Pause. Inhale. Take
the cup to your mouth and sip the tea.

Where did this tea come from? What did it take to
grow the leaves? Think of the hands that raised the
plant, the color of the soil that nourished it. Watch
it as it steams. Swish it around your mouth and let
it warm you. Be present with the beauty.

Sit with your tea and reflect for as long as you like.
You can even brew another cup.

This practice can be adapted for morning coffee in
a French press, too!

PRIORITY
POWER
HOUR

THIS RITUAL IS PERFECT FOR: Reaching your creative goals, feeling less overwhelmed, facing off with procrastination on something important to you.

How many times do you ask someone the question, "How are you?" and get the response, "I am just *so* busy." It's easy to get overwhelmed with the never-ending to-do lists we all keep.

This ritual, inspired by the Pomodoro Technique developed by Francesco Cirillo, will help you focus and complete something important to you. The Priority Power Hour ritual is the secret to getting a significant task done in record time—whether it's creative or business-related. This book was written in a series of Priority Power Hour rituals!

Here's how it works: Work on one priority for fifty minutes, then take a ten-minute break before diving into another fifty-minute block.

Those fifty minutes are all about being focused on what you need to get done. Set a timer to make it feel like a race. When you need to get something done in a set block of time, you will rise to make it happen. Then, for ten minutes, you're on total break, disconnected from all tasks. Doing this, you allow your body and mind to do something else and reset. Extra points if you spend those ten minutes getting your blood flowing with squats or a brisk walk. You may even be able to fit another ritual from the book into the ten minutes.

Ready to get it done? Let's begin.

The first step is to set up your space. To get something done, you need an environment that promotes good work habits. Have whatever you'll need for fifty minutes of uninterrupted work at hand—for example, a pitcher of water and a drinking glass if you usually make frequent trips to the water cooler—and remove distractions. Put your phone on airplane mode, and turn off distracting electronics.

Breathe deeply. Clear your mind of all other tasks—you'll deal with them later. Focus on the one thing you want to achieve. Envision how accomplished you'll feel when the fifty minutes pass.

Set your timer and start! If you feel yourself losing focus, simply take a deep breath and bring your attention back to the work at hand. You'll find fifty minutes pass fast when you're flowing.

After the timer goes off, stop. It's rest time, and of course you can do another cycle if this task isn't quite complete. You don't have to choose fifty-minute increments if it feels better for you to work for twenty-, thirty-, or forty-minute spells.

Doing this on a regular basis will increase your ability to focus and help you achieve your most heartfelt dreams and desires.

WHAT YOU PERCEIVE

TO BE *IN THE WAY* OF

WHAT YOU WANT MOST

MAY BE *THE* WAY.

DIVE DEEPER.

RHYTHM
OF
THE
MOON

THIS RITUAL IS PERFECT FOR: Moving in tandem with nature; connecting with rituals of the ancestral past; reawakening to your primal self; exploring your personal cycles of creativity, strength, and sensuality.

Humans have been worshipping the moon for millennia. It's celebrated as a link between worlds, our wise guide when the sun sleeps, a celestial body gently stirring the tides of the ocean.

Its appearance is ever shifting. Sometimes, all we see is brightness: this symbolizes life. At other times, it is nowhere to be found. The darkness is a symbol of death and rebirth.

The moon is also closely tied to women's menstrual cycles, which may explain why so many ancient moon deities are women, including the Titan Phoebe in Greek mythology, and the goddess Chang'e of Chinese lore—the namesake of that country's first lunar probe. Artemis, the wild Greek goddess of animal life, woodlands, and female independence, was also closely associated with the moon.

The cycle of lunar phases can be a powerful way to set intentions throughout each month. For example, a new moon is the perfect time to create space for the new and make a fresh start. During a full moon, the light can illuminate things that have lingered in the shadows so that you may heal and be complete.

Follow this guide to the moon phases so that you can develop your own rituals around the lunar cycle:

New Moon ritual. The new moon is all about new beginnings. When the light is absent, we have a chance to turn inward and reflect on all the little decisions we make in our life that make us who we are, much like the Write Your Obituary ritual (page 68). As the moon darkens every month, a phase of life dies with it. The new moon is the perfect chance to review and adjust: Are you living in alignment with your core values and the legacy you hope to build?

The ancient Greeks marked the beginning of each new moon phase with a celebration of the god Apollo in sacred spots outside the cities. Apollo, twin brother of the lunar Artemis, is the god of creating order in our lives. He calls us to make our intentions clear and to commit to creating a beautiful life.

His faithful believed that the reverent darkness of the night before a new moon, before the festivities, was a sacred time to give offerings to the gods and make promises for the new cycle.

We can take inspiration from the Greeks and their deep respect for astronomical forces.

During a new moon, find a quiet space in your home and jot down your feelings and thoughts as you begin this new cycle. Think about what you want to invite into your life. What do you want to draw in, in terms of your romantic relationships, your work, your friendships, your time, your home, and your money?

This is a phase of regeneration. When all is dark, you have a chance to reflect on where you've been. This is also the perfect moment to perform other rituals that refer to new beginnings, such as Plant Your Dreams (page 48). This is also a good time for you to revisit your dream journal (page 32) and just sit in contemplation during this dark time. Rest. Reflect and contemplate on what's coming next. Though you do not see the moon and the sky is dark, know something will grow.

More women have their menstrual cycles around the new moon than during any other phase of the moon. This phase is known as the "White Moon Cycle." It's a time for resting, rejuvenating, and recharging, so allow yourself that space as well.

Full Moon ritual. This phase is all about illumination.

This is the moment of the lunar cycle in which the moon shows itself most clearly. It's a majestic sight. This bright moment is one of revelation.

During the full moon, reflect on what is being revealed to you. What has come out of the shadows that needs to be released? Are there any old patterns or wounds that resurface right now? How can you best shed light on them, sit with them, and gently integrate them into your being? The full moon is a good time to be social, so you can either write down your thoughts or talk about them with a friend or a trusted circle.

This is also peak time for sensuality. It's the perfect time to practice rituals like Primal Dance (page 146) and Cleansing Bath (page 44). Tune in to your wildest self and see if, from that place of power, you can expand into whatever the full moon reveals.

Visit discovertherituals.com for a guided moon practice.

BREATHE
IT
OUT

——

THIS RITUAL IS PERFECT FOR: Releasing stress, connecting to your body, developing mindfulness.

Your body breathes, on its own, without any conscious instruction on your part. Your lungs expand and contract with the flow of air, delivering oxygen to your cells, brain, organs, and every part of your body. Take a moment to appreciate your remarkable respiratory system before you dive into this ritual.

It's been proven that mindful breathing, when practiced every day, has enormous benefits, including reducing anxiety, preventing heart disease, improving mental and physical performance, clearing and opening your chakras, and boosting your mood. Ancient yogic breathwork techniques called *pranayama* have been tapping into these benefits for centuries.

Too many of us feel as though we have to wait for our next yoga class, massage, or night alone at home in order to really relax and unwind. That's simply not true. This is a ritual you can do anytime, anywhere. All you need is a timer, somewhere comfortable to sit or stand, and a little music (if you wish).

Let's begin.

Set a timer (with a peaceful alarm tone) for five minutes. If you'd like to play some calming music, put that on.

In a standing or seated position, breathe in deeply for a count of four seconds, and then breathe out deeply for a count of four seconds.

Feel your feet on the floor and your spine in alignment, and relax.

With every inhalation, feel the breath in your body, and with every exhalation, let go of any thoughts occupying your mind or things that are no longer serving you.

If visualizations feel supportive to you in this process, here are two visualizations you can try:

On your inhalation, visualize the core of a ball of light in your heart, and on your exhalation, see that ball of light expanding and filling your heart. This visualization will support you when your heart feels tender, heavy, or closed.

On your inhalation, visualize light pouring through the top of your head, and on your exhalation, move that light down your body and out the bottoms of your feet. Every time you exhale, imagine roots growing downward from your feet, grounding you deep into the earth and her soul. This visualization

will ground you and make you feel strong and
ready for anything that comes your way.

When the timer goes off, you'll feel renewed inside
and out, ready to face the rest of the day.

*Visit discovertherituals.com for a guided breathwork
practice.*

DATE
YOURSELF

———

THIS RITUAL IS PERFECT FOR: Deeping your self-worth, understanding your desires and goals, connecting to your pleasure.

Who says romance needs more than one person? Too often, when we are single, we focus on finding a relationship as fast as we can to avoid being alone and looking at the parts of ourselves that need healing. And when in a relationship, we can get lost in it and begin to lose our personal identity.

Your most important relationship is the one you have with yourself. Taking time to do the things you love and explore the things you desire can be incredibly fulfilling and satisfying. It doesn't matter if you're in a romantic relationship or single—cherishing yourself comes first. As the saying goes, "You cannot pour from an empty cup." In order to fully show up for fulfilling, healthy relationships with others, you need to feel whole and complete yourself.

No other person can make you whole. Only you hold the keys that unlock the most vulnerable layers of your heart. That is why getting to know yourself on a deeper level is essential: only by growing to love yourself, and your shadows, will you be able to accept yourself and others fully.

In this ritual, you will date your luminous self. This practice is all about coming home to yourself and nurturing the most important relationship in your life.

Set aside a block of time in your calendar for this ritual. It can be a morning or afternoon, a whole day, or even a weekend. It can be as simple as a dinner or as extravagant as a whole vacation to yourself. It can be something that you do one time, or, if it's useful to you, it can become a regular habit of self-romance.

During this period, focus on developing a beautiful, nurturing relationship with yourself. A deep knowing that you are whole, perfect, and complete as you are is the greatest gift you will ever get. If you seek this affirmation outside of yourself, you'll spend your life wanting more, more, more—and reaching nothing. The root of an integrated, complete self is—precisely—within the self.

When you fall in love with another person, you want to know everything about them. You want to discover them fully—their desires, their dreams, their fears. It's time to turn that around and get curious about yourself. Here are some questions to get you started:

What would bring me the most joy?
Plan to give yourself exactly that, as if you were wooing yourself.

What would I give as a gift to somebody I love?
Give that to yourself.

Where can I take myself? Where can I make space to just be with myself?
When you have the answer, proceed to take yourself on a date doing whatever you enjoy the most. Think of some questions that you might ask the

other person if you were on a date, and turn those questions back on yourself. Where are you going in life? It's your chance to get curious. Think about what you might want from a date, and give that to yourself.

What have I wanted to receive from another person? Whether it's a tangible thing or a certain behavior or favor, could you give that to yourself?

This is an incredible way not just to unwind, but also to pursue your own passions and spend intentional time doing what matters most to you (which is so easy to forget when you've got a crazy work schedule, a partner, kids, and so on).

During this period, write yourself a love letter. Take yourself out to dinner. Wear sexy undergarments— just to please yourself. Most importantly, do not stop asking questions of yourself. Keep the wonder alive! You are marvelous and full of different, unexplored facets. You don't need someone else to bring them out in you; you can discover yourself for yourself and make your life richer and more fulfilling.

MUSEUM
OF
YOU

THIS RITUAL IS PERFECT FOR: Self-reflection; telling your story; exploring your past, present, and future.

The first known museum in the world dates back to the sixth century B.C.E. It was founded and curated by Princess Ennigaldi of Ur, an ancient Mesopotamian city. The museum provided visitors with a look back on the millennia-long history of the powerful city-empire and helped them make sense of it.

Looking back on our own lives to make sense of them is a natural human tendency. It is in our nature to build a narrative for our lives and document important moments. It's a way for us to give meaning to our stories. This process of documentation is one many people are already actively engaged in through social media, and the intention of this ritual is to bring more presence and truth to the practice.

In a world where a lot of time is spent connecting through social media, we are often carefully crafting a facade: a pretty image that doesn't actually reflect our core. We spend an inordinate amount of time making sure that what we do and what we post get us attention, comments, likes.

This ritual of documentation is completely different. It's about keeping the imprint of what is real, true, present, and alive. This means keeping old journals and photos so you can look back on the cycles of your life and contemplate what has changed. This means recording videos and saving them to a hard drive. This means memorializing the skins that you have shed to be where you are, the layers that you have had to explore to become more whole, more full, more alive.

Set aside one day of the week to work on your self-narrative scrapbook, or if you'd rather, you can do this ritual on special occasions when you want to record something memorable. You don't have to do the same thing every time. You can switch it up with photos, videos, journaling, or whatever captures your experience. The most important piece is to be real with yourself.

Carry the honesty and the essences of this practice into your social media feed and the way you connect with other people. See what unfolds from being more real.

Once a year or when you are at an important crossroads or occasion, like your birthday, spend some time with your documents to review all the lessons learned and track how far you've come.

The true history of yourself is a compass. It teaches you what matters to you, what you have fought for, what you have built. It teaches you that you are strong and resilient enough to find your way, always.

YOUR DESTINY IS
NOT A DESTINATION.
THERE IS NO PLACE
YOU NEED TO GET TO;
ONLY A JOURNEY OF
UNLEARNING AND
LEARNING, UNFURLING
AND EXPANDING.

THEATER
OF
SELF-
DISCOVERY

———

This ritual is the foundation for the rituals
on pages 126 through 137.

THIS RITUAL IS PERFECT FOR: Observing your
behaviors and core patterns, developing self-
awareness, gaining perspective on situations and
relationships.

Do you ever feel yourself getting frustrated or
feeling judgmental toward someone you love
without a clear reason? Do you have a big life
change or major step on the horizon that you feel
unresolved about? Are you hoping to gain insight

into a situation that's been weighing on you? We all experience these feelings from time to time. Our inner landscape is far more complex than we generally realize or acknowledge. This is a good thing—it means there's always more to learn, more to be curious about, more to grow from. But we can only change or be free of things if we have awareness of them.

This ritual will help you observe your behavior and recognize the patterns driving your life. It's also a foundational ritual that can enhance other rituals throughout this book. By taking a closer look at how you show up in relationships, your work, and the world, you will gain new perspectives and a fresh awareness that will allow you to heal and face anything life throws at you.

Let's begin.

Sit in a quiet, undisturbed space with a notebook and a pen.

Imagine you are sitting in a theater, watching scenes from your present life playing out on the screen. As you observe your life, jot down your responses to the following questions:

1. What area of your present life are you most happy with?

2. What area of your present life are you least happy with?

3. How do you perceive yourself looking and feeling?

4. Who is there with you?

5. What positive emotions come up most often?

6. What situations are playing out that trigger those positive emotions?

7. What negative emotions and disempowering thoughts come up most often?

8. What situations are playing out that trigger each of those negative emotions and disempowering thoughts?

9. What do you say and do when experiencing each of the negative emotions and disempowering thoughts?

10. What leaps are you taking?

11. What are you most ashamed of?

12. What do you most desire?

13. What do you most fear?

14. What are you hiding from people?

15. What contribution are you making and how are you making that contribution?

16. What would you change about what you see playing out on the screen? What do you most need or desire that you don't currently have?

17. Anything else you are observing that feels important to note?

Visit discovertherituals.com to download a worksheet for this practice.

RITUAL
OF
THE
MIND

Ritual of the Mind builds on the Theater of Self-Discovery ritual (page 122). In the Theater of Self-Discovery, you were in the audience as an observer, and this ritual will help you step into the director role.

In the last ritual, the Theater of Self-Discovery practice, everything is a projection of your mind. If one of the people you noted from your practice were to do the very same practice, what they perceive could be different than what you perceive. You both have your own story about the situation. Your conditioning, personal experiences, and emotions shape your interpretation of the world, and these interpretations are not necessarily facts. Every one of us contains millions of these big and small meanings about the world and the way we live our lives. We all see and experience the world a little differently, and that can be a beautiful thing.

This is where the empowering practice of questioning your mind comes into play, which isn't an easy feat. Questioning the mind is something humans have done for ages in some form or another. Socrates, the great Greek philosopher, had people question their deep-rooted assumptions through the Socratic Method or Dialogue, which requires taking whatever you believe to be true in your situation and asking critical questions to test your every belief and assumption.

For this ritual, you will need a pen and paper. This practice can take some time, so dive in when you have at least thirty minutes.

First, choose one situation or relationship from the Theater of Self-Discovery that triggers you or brings up a negative emotion or disempowering thought, and put it in statement form. For example, if you observe yourself getting stuck in cycles of procrastination, the statement could be, "I always procrastinate when I have an opportunity to share my ideas." Here's another example: "She doesn't care about me" could be a statement for a relationship with a friend who hasn't been calling you.

Below are some starter questions you can explore as you question your mind, beliefs, assumptions, distortions, and stories. Not all will fit your unique statement and situation, and I invite you to go beyond the questions that are here to expand your awareness. This practice can be done with a friend, too.

What is the meaning you have attached to the belief or thought?

What is your state of being or way of behaving when you choose the belief or thought?

How do you know that? Do you have examples and proof of that? And do you have examples and proof of the contrary?

I invite you to consider that your original statement isn't the truth. For example, if you are considering the statement, "I always procrastinate when I have an opportunity to share my ideas," you should ask yourself, "Do I really *always* procrastinate?" Can you think of times you haven't procrastinated?

How could you look at that differently?

Taking peronal responsibility for your needs, is there anything you are waiting for someone else to give you that you can give yourself right now?

I invite you to explore any ways you don't show care for yourself. For example, if you are exploring the statement, "She doesn't care about me," consider what you can do for yourself to feel more cared for and loved.

Asking yourself a series of questions will let you more clearly perceive how you are automatically processing (and, perhaps, distorting) your view of a situation or relationship to fit a vision of reality that might not be true.

This ritual plants a seed for questioning your mind. It's about developing greater awareness, which gives you the personal power to get to choose differently.

Now you have a tool for questioning your assumptions and judgments. You get to start talking back to that voice in your head. You get to talk back to those judgments, the guilt, the shame, the behaviors that are not serving you. You get to respond to the world from a place of power instead of reacting from a place of fear.

IMAGO
DIALOGUE

THIS RITUAL IS PERFECT FOR: Developing conscious communication in relationships; resolving conflict; learning how to be seen and heard, and doing the same for others.

Once you've completed the Theater of Self-Discovery (page 122) and Ritual of the Mind (page 126), you will likely be aware of any challenges in a relationship that means a lot to you. The Imago Dialogue is a practice developed by therapists Harville Hendrix and Helen Hunt that has become an essential part of all my relationships. I invite you to dive deeper into their teachings. This ritual will improve and expand your relationship with a partner, as well as your inner consciousness, in a myriad of ways. It facilitates positive, nourishing communication and supports you in creating intimate, loving relationships.

The Imago Dialogue is based on the principle that everyone lives their own reality, as we explored in Ritual of the Mind: Your reality is perceived to be the truth and valid, while other people's realities are their truths and also valid. Can you see how that principle creates some issues and tension, especially in our relationships? It can be easy to lose sight of this when conflicts erupt. That's when we slip into a tendency to put up walls to protect ourselves, which can make it harder to accept someone else's reality as valid.

The Imago Dialogue is all about shifting perceptions away from that tight place of self-preservation and back to a place of mutual recognition and acceptance.

This ritual can be helpful when you and your partner are working through issues, as well as when you simply need to check in with one another. Consider putting it on the calendar as a communication date every week or month.

Here's how it goes:

Designate one person as the Listener and one person as the Speaker. These roles will likely depend on the situation you're discussing. Together you will move through the dialogue in three steps: mirroring, validation, and empathy.

Mirroring. First, the Listener listens mindfully to what the Speaker expresses. Then, the Listener reflects back to them what they interpreted from what they said, getting clarification on anything not understood. Do this without giving your opinion on what the Speaker said; simply paraphrase to check there are no misunderstandings.

Validation. Next, the Speaker validates what the Listener said to confirm agreement. If any parts did not make sense, the Speaker can clarify and express more.

Empathy. Finally, the Listener reflects back to the Speaker how what's being expressed is making the Speaker feel. In this part it's essential to remember that feelings are different from thoughts. Don't get into deep analysis and complex opinions. Rather, describe feelings in a few words.

This is about empathy: working to put yourself in the other person's shoes and understand their feelings from the inside.

After these steps have been completed, the roles can be switched (although it may feel complete with only one person sharing). This creates a safe space for feelings and emotions to be expressed and acknowledged.

This practice will develop habits of empathetic listening during moments of tension, as well as in moments of deep connection. Lean into it and listen to one another; you will be stronger, more connected, and more deeply understood.

TRAVEL
THROUGH
TIME

THIS RITUAL IS PERFECT FOR: Holding big dreams and visions for your life, goal setting, getting clarity on what you truly want.

In this time-travel ritual, we are going to revisit the Theater of Self-Discovery (page 122). This time, though, you are going to sit and watch your life playing out in the future.

It could be three months from now, a year from now, five years from now. I recommend focusing on a year from now for the purpose of this exercise. However, the choice is yours.

Get a pen and paper and sit in your sacred space or a quiet spot. Breathe, clear your mind, and start!

Visualize your life in your chosen time frame. Make the details as vivid as you can; include all of your senses and emotions. Take as long as you need to do this.

Write down what you are seeing, hearing, and feeling as you watch this epic story of what's possible for you in your life.

Contemplate these questions as you unleash your imagination:

If it all paid the same, what would you be doing?

What if you remembered that you cannot fail?

What do you really want?
Dream big and be specific.

What will you see and hear and
feel when you have what you want?

How will you know when you
have what you want?

What will having what you want give you?

For what purpose do you want it?

What positive contribution do you
want to make to the world?

How will you make that contribution?

Who, exactly, will you make
that contribution for?

What is a leap in that direction that
you can take right now?

Write down anything else you see, sense, and feel.
When you're done, you can use the next ritual to
write a letter to this future version of you, or burn
the page while holding intention in your heart.

TURN

"ONE DAY"

INTO

DAY ONE.

LETTER
TO YOUR
FUTURE
SELF

THIS RITUAL IS PERFECT FOR: Mapping out your goals, discovering who you want to expand into, self-reflection, reconnecting to your past and future.

One of the most powerful things we can do for ourselves is find creative ways to commit to our goals. The more real, powerful, and possible we make them feel, the more likely we are to achieve them.

In this ritual you'll write a letter to your future self. When you're creating something new or dreaming of a big change, it is a powerful practice to sit down to write future you a letter as if you were writing to a dear friend: pouring out your hopes, visions, and wishes for the future.

To begin this ritual, quiet your mind and focus. Think about yourself at a point in the future. It may be a specific date you have in mind, or the completion of a goal or big milestone in your life like graduating, getting married, or starting a new job.

Who will you be?

What will you have?

What did it take for you to get there?

How did the journey feel?

What did you learn about
yourself on the journey?

What advice or words of encouragement
do you have for your future self?

After you've reflected on these questions, begin writing.

Speak to this radiant, beautiful future you. Express how much you love future you, and what you're doing now to make sure that future you has a beautiful and rich life.

Seal the letter with a clear "Do not open until [X date]," and place it somewhere safe and memorable.

When you read it, you'll be able to remember the person you were when it all began. It's a magical, soul-stirring way to remain connected to your vision and the past versions of yourself who got you to where you are.

MAKE
BEAUTIFUL
MEMORIES
FOR YOUR
FUTURE SELF
TODAY.

THE
BEING
BOARD

———

THIS RITUAL IS PERFECT FOR: Embodying your deepest truth and desires, confidence, expressing yourself more fully.

This ritual is like a vision board for the way you are showing up in the world right now. But while a vision board is often about what you want in the future and the things you'll *do*, your "being board" is about who you are being *now*; it's about embodying your deepest desires and the essences that are at the core of the path you are blazing down toward your future.

First, you'll want to have a large piece of paper or foam board and magazines, images, glue, and markers.

Choose five essences from the list below that feel aligned with who you want to *be* in the world, in your work, in your relationships. What you are embodying can definitely be aligned with future goals, but the focus is on acting on the future *now*. For example, let's say you really want to build a successful business around your creative passions. Start embodying the qualities of a successful business owner now. How does a successful business owner act and move through the day? You may choose the essences "bravery," "hustle," "leadership," "organization," and "abundance" to play with and embody.

Below is a list of essences to get you started. Put these words on your piece of paper or board or even a wall, and cut out images that express the words and how you want to feel and be right now, in this moment. Have fun with it.

Abundance	Aliveness
Activism	Artistry
Adventure	Beauty
Alignment	Bravery

Chaos	Intimacy
Connection	Knowing
Courage	Leadership
Creativity	Liberation
Divine Mother	Love
Divinity	Luxury
Ecstasy	Magic
Empowerment	Magnetism
Expansion	Organization
Femininity	Overflow
Fire	Passion
Forward motion	Playfulness
Freedom	Possibility
Fulfillment	Power
Generosity	Presence
Grace	Queen
Gratitude	Radiance
Hustle	Receptivity
Imagination	Self-expression
Impact	Sensuality
Innovation	Service
Inspiration	Sexuality

Simplicity	Wealth
Strength	Wellness
Truth	Wonder
Visibility	Worthiness
Wanderlust	

Put your Being Board somewhere you will see it often as a reminder that your future is being created right now, and that you can achieve and bring to life anything you embody. How you choose to be will determine what you see.

PRIMAL
DANCE

———

THIS RITUAL IS PERFECT FOR: Exploring your most creative self, embodying radical self-expression, unlocking potent personal freedom.

Dance has played an important role in religions and cultures around the world. The *volva*, or Norse seeress, would dance by the fire and rock back and forth, or even roll on the ground, until she reached a state of trance. Then the old gods spoke to her, and she traveled the nine worlds of Norse mythology as if flying.

From the Maasai dance to mark becoming a warrior to the celebratory and spirited dance of the San tribe in Botswana, dance is a major aspect of rituals, ceremonies, and community in African cultures.

Research on how dance impacts the brain shows there may be more profound benefits. Recent studies have shown that dancing regularly can help strengthen your brain's ability to move more smoothly and solve problems, help you stay attuned to your surroundings, and can even help prevent depression.

Our bodies want to move and express from the inside out. Join me in returning to our magical roots.

Put on a playlist you love to move or dance to. If you don't have one ready to go, you can use any music app to create your own or pick one that already exists. It doesn't have to sound like conventional dance music—for this ritual it's best if you go with your gut feeling, so choose whatever you like. You can also try a traditional dance from your culture and see what awakens in you.

To make this dance a very intentional practice, choose an essence from The Being Board ritual (page 142) to embody during your dance. Dance that essence into your entire being. If the essence is ecstasy, how do you move when *being* ecstasy? What does dancing in ecstasy look and feel like?

Move your entire body. There's no judgment here. Be wild and primal. Let go.

Those are, really, the only instructions. There is no right or wrong way to dance—simply do it from the heart. Don't think of what it looks like, just flow.

If you want to ease into this ritual or try it in another form, here is a variation:

Sit on the floor and start rocking your torso back and forth. After a minute, begin crawling around on the floor.

As you begin to feel more loose, roll and sway your hips, the center of your sensuality. Shake your body gently.

Start moving your arms, hands, and shoulders, and let every part of your body move naturally to the beat. Start to stretch your face, close your eyes, open your mouth and smile, laugh, or sing along to the music. Pretend you're someone or something else: a lion, a mermaid, a rainbow, a tree. It doesn't matter.

Let it go. Let it all happen at once. Anything you're holding on to can be released this way. Don't numb yourself to anything. Let your body move however it wants to and express any feeling or emotion coming up.

Whether you want to be sensual, or jump around, or move like an animal—let yourself be free.

NO-THING
AND
NONATTACHMENT

––––––––

THIS RITUAL IS PERFECT FOR: Identifying what you really want and what you don't, feeling deeply grateful.

In life, work, and love, many of us are subconsciously driven by the desire for more. More experiences. More money. More attention or affection from our partner or those around us.

And it's no wonder: we live in a world where we're served hundreds of ads and marketing materials that encourage us to think of "more" as the goal.

But when was the last time you asked for nothing, no-thing, at all?

There is something incredibly healing about making a ritual of counting your blessings instead of constantly seeking new ones. It is a beautiful thing to be able to follow our dreams and passions without being attached to outcomes.

In the Sanskrit scripture the *Bhagavad Gita*, we find this concept depicted masterfully. It is called *anasakti yoga*: the practice of nonattachment to the material world. It doesn't mean you don't care. Rather, this practice separates *You* from your actions and their material results. It's about centering on the core of your being instead of pursuing external events.

Rather than focusing on the things you don't have but desire, consider what you already have. Spend a day in this zone, wishing for nothing, and instead giving and expressing gratitude.

This is a small and simple ritual to increase gratitude and hold space for what you already have. It's ideal for those days when you feel you need that new device, pair of shoes, or haircut, or even a new partner, group of friends, or professional life. It's perfect for when you find yourself so fixated on a destination or expectation that you forget to enjoy the journey and what is real in the present moment.

Let's begin.

Count to four as you breathe in, choosing to feel gratitude for something or someone in your life.

Hold your breath in for four seconds and dwell on what that person or thing fills you with. Use your imagination to picture this vividly.

Exhale that gratitude for four seconds, visualizing it surrounding the person or thing with bright light and appreciation in the present moment.

Let your lungs be empty for four seconds, dwelling in gratitude as you complete the cycle.

Repeat this cycle as many times as you wish. You can repeat the same focus or choose a different person or thing every time.

Dwell in gratitude as you hold the breath at the bottom of the exhalation for four seconds. There is always something beautiful to see.

Maybe you find that what you thought you needed is no longer necessary. Maybe you still feel you want it—but, now, it's not a compulsion to fill an inner void. This doesn't mean you shouldn't treat yourself or desire new things, but what you do consume should be done mindfully and add to your joy, not to your worry or insecurity. This ritual will help you choose things carefully, from a place of joy and love, and provide you with a tool to let go of unhealthy attachments.

THE
ULTIMATE
RITUAL

———

As we come to the end of this book, I want you to remember this:

You being here, having this human experience and expressing spirit in a way that is uniquely your own, is a miracle to celebrate and honor every day. The rituals we practice are ways to honor our existence, experiences, and the cycles we move through.

I wrote this book in many different places and through many seasons of life. I wrote it through moving and settling in a new country. I wrote it through heartache and then falling madly in love. I wrote in the depths of pain and in ecstatic bliss. These practices have been ever-present, and I hope they will be for you now, too.

I want you to continue to relish in these rituals and practices like the sacred acts they are. Continue to revisit them and unlock new parts of yourself. Return to these practices to drop into a state of deep presence, and then bring that to as many seconds, minutes, and hours of your days as you can.

If you find that a ritual becomes rigid or boring, or if you feel yourself beginning to resist it, add your own spin on it or simply let it go. Make space for new practices in new seasons of life.

Live by what makes you feel alive.

Live by play.

Live by your expansion as a spiritual being having this wild, messy, beautiful human experience.

YOU ARE THE RITUAL.

**THE END IS SIMPLY WHERE
WE BEGIN AGAIN.**

Download guided practices from *The Rituals*.

Connect to our community.

Attend a life-changing retreat.

Reveal your purpose.

Begin at discovertherituals.com.

G
R
A
T
I
T
U
D
E

It truly feels like this book has been years in the
works, going as far back as my childhood, when
I made circles and labyrinths out of stones and
flowers. It was a practice that came naturally and
made me feel more connected to the world around
me. Many years later, during a solo trip to England,
I participated in a group ritual that was strikingly
similar to this childhood practice, and something
shifted inside me during that shared experience. I
am so grateful to all the people I've connected with
through ritual over the years.

To my agent, Melissa Flashman, thank you for
being my creative partner for three books now and
for believing in this book from the moment I shared
it with you a few years ago in that little café in
Brooklyn.

My editorial team is incredible. Rachel Hiles, I
could not have asked for a better editor for this
project, and I'm grateful you gave it a home at
Chronicle Books. Hillary Weiss, your editorial
guidance and creative support is always appreci-
ated. Desiree Adaway, thank you for your input as
I reflected on the responsibility I hold in sharing
these practices with reverence and appreciation.
Lindsay Hine, your artwork elevates this book and
captures my vision so perfectly, and Vanessa Dina,
you were a dream designer to work with to pull it
all together.

Layla Martin, from the edge of the mountaintop in Sequoia National Park to lying under the Milky Way in the Namibian desert to our Burning Man sunrise, we've shared so many amazing ritual experiences together that I am reverently grateful for. Thank you for being my biggest cheerleader.

To my love, I'm getting a sweet message from you as I type this. You helped me access a well of creativity as I was finishing this book. Thank you.

I believe it's important to honor our teachers and the people we learn from. I have many—from those I've done in-person trainings with to others I've never met in person to dear friends I can have meaningful conversations and discuss profound ideas with. Thank you for touching my life and my work, and for helping me connect to the truth of who I am and who we are: Alexi Panos, Layla Martin, Alyssa Nobriga, Steve Linder, Osho, Guru Singh, Siri Kartar, Byron Katie, Harville Hendrix,

Helen Hunt, Ken Wilber, Wakuha, Latham Thomas, Thich Nhat Hanh, Susan Bushell, Punnu Wasu, Sally Kempton, Nisha Moodley, Sabrina Mesko, Aaron Alexander, Sarah Anne Stewart, Diana House, Desiree Adaway, and Marianne Williamson. If you're a teacher or friend who isn't named here, I honor you for the role you've played in my life and expansion.

And to you, dear reader, thank you for being on this journey with me and sharing *The Rituals* so widely. I bow to you.

NATALIE MACNEIL is an Emmy Award–winning media entrepreneur listed on the Levo 100 as a transformer of her generation and featured by *Inc.* as one of 27 women leaders changing the world. Devoted to expanding human potential and inspiring people to live deeply meaningful lives, she has produced three interactive film experiences, written three bestselling books, and created the popular website She Takes on the World, which was listed by *Forbes* as one of the "100 Best Websites for Women." She has been featured in *Elle*, *Glamour*, *People*, *TIME*, *Forbes*, *Inc.*, *Entrepreneur*, and more.

CONNECT WITH NATALIE:
Website: nataliemacneil.com
Instagram: @nataliemacneil
Facebook: nataliemacneil
YouTube: NatalieMacNeilTV

Chronicle Books publishes distinctive books and gifts. From award-winning children's titles, best-selling cookbooks, and eclectic pop culture to acclaimed works of art and design, stationery, and journals, we craft publishing that's instantly recognizable for its spirit and creativity. Enjoy our publishing and become part of our community at **www.chroniclebooks.com.**